THE GARDEN OF ENGLAND

FROM THE AIR

THE GARDEN OF ENGLAND
FROM THE AIR

JASON HAWKES

TED SMART

This edition produced for The Book People Ltd, Hall Wood Avenue, Haydock, St Helens WA11 9UL

1 3 5 7 9 10 8 6 4 2

First published by Ebury Press

Random House, 20 Vauxhall Bridge Road, London SW1V 2SA

Random House Australia (Pty) Limited
20 Alfred Street, Milsons Point, Sydney, New South Wales 2061, Australia

Random House New Zealand Limited
18 Poland Road, Glenfield, Auckland 10, New Zealand

Random House (Pty) Limited
Endulini, 5a Jubilee Road, Parktown 2193, South Africa

The Random House Group Limited Reg. No. 954009

www.randomhouse.co.uk

Papers used by Ebury Press are natural, recyclable products made
from wood grown in sustainable forests.

A CIP catalogue record for this book is available from the British Library

ISBN 0 09 187907 8

Text by Adele McConnel

Designed by David Fordham

Typeset in Trajan and Fournier by MATS, Southend-on-Sea, Essex
Printed and bound in Portugal

Photograph on page 2: Leeds Castle

CONTENTS

INTRODUCTION
THE GARDEN OF ENGLAND

Five and twenty ponies
Trotting though the dark —
Brandy for the parson,
'Baccy for the clerk;
Laces for a lady, letters for a spy,
And watch the wall, my darling, while the Gentlemen go by!
RUDYARD KIPLING

Y OU WOULD BE HARD PUSHED to find a more eventful place than the south-east coast of England. The water here has resulted in its constant use as a gateway to the whole country, and for centuries everyone from invading forces to (rather more welcome) tourists have been using it as such. We, however, are going to use a different element to explore the aptly named Garden of England – the air. Intended as neither a guidebook nor a history lesson, the book does, unapologetically, mix a little of both. But its true purpose is to capture a rarely seen view of the south-east, and explore the region's rich history, personality and complex texture to its best advantage.

Our photographer Jason Hawkes is a pro at this, of course. With a plethora of books and advertising campaigns under his belt, he can snap commercial images or turn everyday objects into inscrutable patterns with the click of a button. Appreciation of aerial photography, however, seems to have been relatively recent. Edward Steichen, a painter as well as a photographer, wrote in 1918 that prints taken from the air were 'as uninteresting and unimpressive a picture as can be imagined (because) it badly represents nature from an angle we do not know'. Ten years later, in 1929, the same point was argued the opposite way by Werner Graff, who noted 'The rules of central perspective have in any event never been applied to aerial photography. Verticals do not become vertical, and yet the pictures are attractive and one's pleasure is not impaired because they do not conform to the well-established rules of perspective.' The reality seems to be that pleasure is enhanced by discovering new ways of looking at familiar objects.

One magazine article on Jason Hawkes described what he does for a living as 'flirting with fear', and having flown with him many times over the years, I am inclined to agree with the author of that piece. Hanging out of a Jet Ranger helicopter with the door taken off, at heights of up to 2,000 feet, may all be in a day's work for our photographer, but this

WHITE CLIFFS AND BOATS

The history and character of the whole of the south-east corner of England have been formed by its long

coastline facing the English Channel, and its dependence on the sea for trade and commerce.

author is much happier at her PC! Undeniable, however, is not only the surprising sense of freedom at such a height, but also the sheer awe at the breathtaking views that confront you. Not only are mundane sights transformed into interesting puzzles pieces, but the contrasts in the scenery that this region is famed for – from the coastline, to the marshes, to the fields, forests and orchards – become abundantly clear.

Sussex, Kent and Hampshire are counties shaped by their history and so firmly entwined in their past that you can not separate the two. No introduction to this area would be complete without at least a mention of the Battle of Hastings in 1066 and the notorious murder of Thomas Becket in Canterbury in the next century. From William the Conqueror to Hitler, the coastline has always been the first port of call for wanted and unwanted visitors, and it still bears the scars of successive invasions in the form of castles and forts. Most famous of all invasions must be the one by Julius Caesar in AD 55, and after losing the battle, again the year after. In AD 43, the Romans landed here, led by Aulus Plautius, leaving in their wake a massive concentration of Roman shore-castles. Later, Hengist and Horsa, responsible for the White Horse Symbol amongst other things, led the Anglo-Saxons to this coast; and when the Normans landed here they built a mass of mighty fortresses such as those at Rochester, Dover and Canterbury. The locations for these buildings were so obviously appropriate to their purpose that future generations very often incorporated ruined remains into new castle structures.

Today the coastline is still used as an access point for overseas visitors, with a busy passenger ferry port at Dover, and hydrofoils from Folkestone and the Channel Tunnel whisking people over the seas in a matter of hours. However, as such a susceptible place for invasion it has had to be built up as the first line of defence. The first major step was the creation of the Cinque Ports to prevent, in the first instance, Danish Intruders. Built during the 13th century, many medieval kings depended on these ports to provide ships and men should the need for defence arise. The original ports were Hastings, Sandwich, Dover, Romney and Hythe; the ancient towns of Winchelsea and Rye were later added, as were around 30 other towns. In return for their allegiance to the King, these ports were granted many privileges, such as exemption from tax, the right to levy tolls and to local self-government, the authority to 'punish shedders of blood and seize those who fled from justice' and the authority to compel holders of stolen goods to divulge their source.

The last privilege was no doubt aimed at combating the growing smuggling problem, immortalised by Kipling's poem (above), and made possible by the shore's wealth of accommodating and secluded inlets. When the exportation of wool from England was prohibited to protect the weaving trade, many farmers overproduced at a price too low to make a decent profit. The answer was to start a black market and smuggle the wool to the continent, where there was a great demand for it. Smuggling was not confined to wool, however. All kinds of products were smuggled into England, from brandy and rum to lace, jewellery and tea. By the 1660s the death penalty was imposed for anyone caught smuggling wool, and firearms were introduced to try and reduce the problem. Unfortunately, this actually had the opposite effect and by the end of the 17th century carrying a firearm was considered commonplace. There are literally hundreds of stories about famous smuggling gangs, such as the Hawkhurst and North Kent gangs. One of my favourites happened in 1817 when George Snelling, himself the son of the notorious 'Broadstairs Smuggler' Joss Snelling, arrived aboard a smuggling vessel at Dumpton Gap. Having waited for, but not seen, a signal from the beach he carefully crept ashore and was confronted by seven abandoned horses at the top of the cliff. It transpired that seven revenue men had lain in wait for him at the foot of the cliffs, and had been buried alive by a landslide.

Smuggling died out in the 1800s for two main reasons. The defeat of Napoleon meant there were additional ships to carry out coastal blockades, and additional men were available to take on a kind of coastguard role. Secondly, the gradual improvements to roads increased the amount of traffic, saw the end to relied-upon secret forest tracks and made it difficult for the owlers (so-called either because they usually worked at night, or because they communicated by hooting to each other) to carry out their trade.

Nowadays the coast is more famous for the gleaming white hulks of the Dover Cliffs and the impressive stretches of golden-sanded beaches. From the air, you get a very sharp realisation of just how much these seaside resorts contrast with the rest of the countryside. 5,000 years ago, just behind the Sussex coast, Stone Age man grazed his sheep on the South Downs, and even today these green slopes produce sheep that are exported all over the world. (As you can imagine, this was a popular place with smugglers!) As for how the Downs look, Kipling describes it more vividly than I ever could, 'blunt, bowheaded, whale-backed'. As well as the empty acres of Pevensey Levels and Romney Marshes, where solitary sheep graze among disused relics from the past, there are the eerie north Kent marshes, seemingly barren of people or landmarks.

The Garden of England is not a term used lightly. As well as cultivated and well-maintained gardens such as Sissinghurst, Kent, Sussex and Hampshire are inhabited by every colour of green imaginable. The steep banks of the North and South Downs face each other inwards across the Weald. This was once covered in deep forest, but is today a countryside full of enchanting villages, splendid mansions, rich farms, fruit-bearing orchards and hop gardens with conical oast houses. And when I say enchanting, I mean it. From wonderful place names like the Devil's Punch Bowl, chiselled out of the hillsides by rain and wind over the centuries, to the allegedly magical Wealden forests of St Leonards and Ashdown where deer run wild, everywhere you go there is a legend or a story to be told. For example, legend has it that Silent Pool, one mile west of Shere, is so called because King John frightened a peasant girl bathing there (quite how has been lost to history), who fell in and drowned. More recent stories include the notorious 'discovery' of a skull in Piltdown by Charles Dawson, a solicitor and amateur antiquarian, in 1912. It was regarded as a missing link between ape and man, about 150,000 years old, until 1953, when it was shown to be a hoax that had been contrived by adding the jaw and canine tooth of a modern ape to fragments of a genuine 50,000-year-old human skull.

In Chertsey, a curfew bell in the church commemorates Blanch Heriot. Her story goes that during the Wars of the Roses her lover was to be executed at curfew. To prevent this, she climbed the church tower and hung on the clapper of the bell, until he was reprieved. Her courage inspired the ballad 'Curfew Must Not Ring Tonight' by the American poet Rose Hartwick Thorpe.

In fact, the Garden of England has inspired more than just a ballad. It has inspired monumental castles and houses, such as Knole House and Ightham Mote. It has inspired thousands of men to fight for king and country. It has inspired stories and legends by the dozen and it has inspired some fine English literature; Dickens lived and wrote in Kent, Defoe wrote Robinson Crusoe at Cranbrook, Kipling wrote of 'the wooded, dim, blue goodness of the Weald', and G.K. Chesterton and Hilaire Belloc sang the praises of Sussex.

But don't take my word for it, or theirs. With a bit of luck, when you turn the pages of this book, filled to the brim with unusual perspectives on an everyday world, you will discover for yourself the qualities that make the Garden of England so inspiring.

ADELE MCCONNEL

RURAL

Despite its relatively high level of population, the Garden of England is still an area dense with fields, woodland and forests. There are many beautiful gardens open to the public, such as Sissinghurst, some of which are seen later in this book. These rural qualities play an important role in forming the landscape and personality of the south-east of England, and have done for centuries. For example The Weald, stretching between the North and South Downs, was covered in thick forest during Saxon times and its name is derived from the Saxon term wald, meaning forest. The suffixes – hurst (meaning wood) and –den (meaning clearing) are commonly found in village names around the area.

The photographs that follow show a stark contrast between the thick, luscious greenery and the surrounding eerie sheep-speckled marshes. In Roman times, the Romney and Denge marshes were actually submerged beneath the English Channel. The lowering of sea levels in the Middle Ages created a 40-square-mile area of marshland, which was affected by malaria and other diseases until the 19th century.

From sheep farming to fruit growing, inhabitants have had to work the land for one reason above all others – the need to eat. For these coastal counties, fishing has histrocially been a major industry; oysters from Whitstable and the famous Dover sole are two local varieties that spring immediately to mind. But the area is perhaps most famous for hops, which have been grown in Kent for centuries. Introduced by the Romans, they used to be eaten as a vegetable. Until hops were introduced to the brewing process, the British drank ale made from malt, honey and herbs, but they soon grew to love the bitter flavour the hops provided. The climate and soil in Kent makes it suitable for another type of alcoholic drink, a light German type of wine. Cider-making was also popular here and was probably introduced in the 12th century from France, although it soon spread to the West Country.

Hop-picking was once extremely labour intensive: the vine produces new shoots each spring which can grow up to 25 feet long, and so have to be wound around a framework of poles. Once upon a time people had to balance on stilts to carry this out, but today tractors are fitted with chair lifts, simplifying the process somewhat. Indeed, technological advances have also changed the look of the landscape, from the creation of ruler-straight lines across the fields to the cessation of the need for dewponds and windmills.

OAST HOUSES AND GROOMBRIDGE PLACE

Left Although today many of the oasthouses have been demolished or converted into homes, hops were once an important crop in this area. The round oasthouses, with their cone shaped roofs, were used for drying the hops ready for the beer brewing process. The bittersweet smell of hops drying in the kilns once pervaded the surrounding area. The simple tractor lines show how far technological advances have come in the world of farming. *Above* Groombridge Place, in Kent, is a delightful 17th-century manor house.

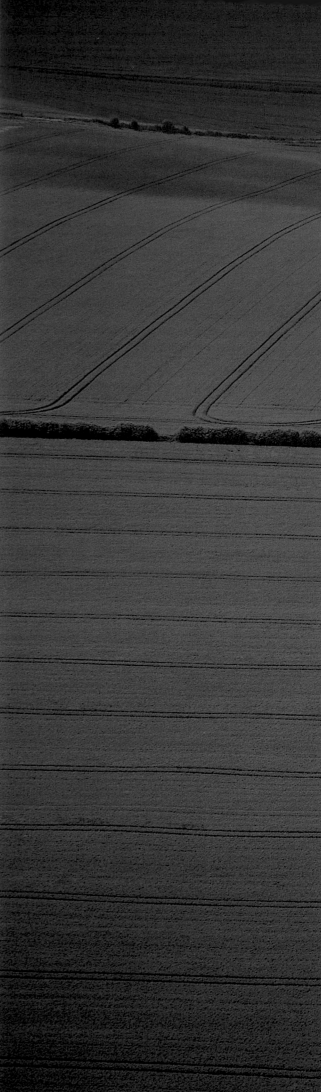

FIELDS

Just as our photographer Jason Hawkes uses a Global Positioning Satellite to pinpoint the position of his photographs, so too can farmers. It is now possible to commission an infra-red aerial survey of a farm, to ascertain which parts are producing the highest yield. GPS waypoints are then downloaded onto high-tech fertiliser spreaders, so that the farmer can decide on the quantity of fertiliser to use.

CLAYTON AND GOODWOOD

The parish church at Clayton contains a series of 12th-century wall murals, thought to be by the same group of artists responsible for those at Hardham and Coombes. The murals depict scenes of eternal damnation from the Last Judgement, and were rediscovered in the 1890s. The twin 19th-century windmills pictured here stand above the village on Clayton Hill, and are known locally as Jack and Jill.

Above Another windmill, near Goodwood, set in remote countryside. The heyday of windmills was between the 12th and early 19th centuries but their demise was brought about by the next step in technology, the development of steam power. However, interest was revived in the 1970s when renewable sources of energy became an increasingly attractive proposition.

A CROP CIRCLE

Above These often complex formations, usually found in wheat or barley fields, have been attributed over the years to everything from hoaxes to plasma vortexes, not to mention supernatural or extra-terrestrial attempts at communication. Perhaps there is a natural explanation, as crop circles often appear on ley lines and occur over underground water supplies or land situated above chalk beds. In recent years 'artists' have come forward claiming responsibility for this phenomenon. There are many reports of physical side effects such as nausea or giddiness in people who have visited crop circles, as well as electronical equipment failing. Luckily for our photographer, neither of these effects occurred with him!

A DEW POND NEAR THE A27

Right In pre-historic times, the climate was much wetter than it is today, but over the centuries the Downs were turned into waterless uplands as the countryside slowly dried up. The hills, being of porous chalk, could not hold moisture, so farmers would collect water on their roofs or build large wells. From the 17th century, this drying-up process led to the creation of shallow, man-made hollows, usually between 20 or 30 feet across. Maintained more by rainwater than dew, these ponds finally became redundant when livestock were supplied with water through troughs linked to main water supplies, and today there are few remaining.

16

FOREST, FIELDS AND WOODS

Like the canopy of an Amazonian rain forest, the image of the green wood looks very fresh and luscious. Over the last few hundred years, however, much of the woodland that once appeared in Britain has been felled and it is only with the benefit of hindsight that we begin to realise what a mistake that was. Similarly the modern farming methods employed nowadays shape our countryside in such a way that our ancestors would never be able to reconcile what they might see now with what they knew then. Geometric patterns that could only be man-made now cover our countryside, and viewed from the air are often difficult to identify.

FIELDS

At a cost of over £100,000 for a new combine harvester, farmers need at least 400 acres of cereal in order to justify such a huge expense. These enormous machines can cover 4 to 6 acres an hour, so often small-scale farms will contract out the harvesting to specialist contractors.

MARSHES NEAR LYDD AIRPORT

As the nearest British airport to France, Lydd runs a daily scheduled service to Le Touquet. Offering European regional carriers access to one of the fastest expanding regions of Europe, and catering mainly for private flights, Lydd airport is notoriously hard to see from the air. These marshes are just down the road.

FIELDS

Here is a more archetypal image of the English countryside: fields of grass and cereals, and the winding network of hedgerows full of wildlife. Patterns such as these have been created over generations of local farming communities, since the enclosures in the 18th century.

POPPY FIELDS AND STUBBLE BURNING

In the language of flowers, poppies can mean either consolation or extravagance. They are unusual flowers in that the seeds can lie dormant for years, and then suddenly germinate, usually due to a disturbance in the earth, such as road works or building sites. They are becoming rarer as agricultural chemical sprays prohibit their growth, but they certainly add a vivid splash of colour to the greenery of the fields.

Stubble burning (*right*). Although now outlawed, this process kills any lurking bugs, and the ashes are ploughed back into the soil acting as a fertiliser for the new crops.

FRUIT TREES

The strictly regimented pattern in these two images is a result of modern farming methods. By planting the fruit trees in lines, tractors are granted easy access for crop spraying and picking. Although today so much of our food is imported, Kent especially is still an important supplier of much of Britain's fruit. Since Tudor times apples, pears, plums and cherries have been grown here, and during the summer months many students and travellers find seasonal employment fruit picking. Cherry production has declined during the last half century, due to its labour intensive production, but apples such as Cox and Bramley continue to thrive.

Hops Fields

Hops were first used as a medicinal herb in early Egypt, and then later in Europe to treat liver disease and digestive complaints. It was not until the 15th century that hops became used for brewing, when weavers from Flanders settled in Kent to benefit from the area's prosperous wool industry. With them, they brought new varieties of hops and the knowledge of how to use them, although several centuries passed before it became accepted in traditional brewing techniques. Today there are around 200 hop farmers, with the fields measuring a total of 7,630 acres across Oxfordshire, Herefordshire, Hampshire, Worcestershire and the South East.

GREENHOUSES

You could probably keep guessing for a year before identifying the picture above

as rows of greenhouses, laid out in even more structured rows than the hops.

HISTORY

SINCE THE FRENCH COAST is so near to this part of Britain, the south-east of England was for many centuries the first line of defence against foreign invasion. It is unsurprising, therefore, that the strategic importance of this area has led to a high concentration of castles. On the other hand, since the Norman Conquest few of these castles ever saw battle, which was just as well since most of them were built as stately homes. From the reign of Henry II (1154-89), noblemen were not allowed to build castles without direct permission from the King. However, they continued to want to do so for the added prestige. Consequently, the emphasis for many castles was on luxury and comfort, rather than on defence. A good example of this is Hermonceux, it's name derived from the love tryst between a Saxon lady called Idonea de Herst and a Norman nobleman Ingelram de Monceux. As it was never put to the military test, much of the original remains.

Each wave of newcomers tried to build defences against the next, and the sites have been passed through many generations, all of whom, from the Romans to the present day, have left some trace of their occupation. One very notable exception to this is the first photograph over the page, the Long Man of Wilmington. No one knows when, why or by whom this monument was created, although over the years there have been many theories. Its purpose has been attributed to marking the location of buried treasure, forecasting the weather, and being a solar almanac, as well as having powers of fertility. Theories put forward as to the man's identity include everything from an inscription of a pilgrim to a god or a hero such as Woden, Baldur or Thor. Depending on which story you choose to believe, the two staves he holds might be either a rake and a scythe or the gates of heaven. Perhaps the monks from the nearby village cut it, for either amusement or heretical reasons; or perhaps, as one legend has it, this is the memorial of a real giant, an outline of where he died.

From the Long Man, to the castles, to the recently created mazes, the photographs in this section of the book skim through some of the most conspicuous monuments of this area, and in doing so slice across 2,000 years of a history packed with battles, murder, mystery and legend.

THE LONG MAN OF WILMINGTON AND LEEDS CASTLE

Left Whatever its real purpose, origin or age, the best view of the Long Man, or Giant, of Wilmington really is from the air. Carved into the chalk and standing 230 feet high, this enigmatic figure has fascinated people for years. But only an aerial view can demonstrate that the carving has been carried out so painstakingly that its proportions are true to life.

(*Above*) Leeds Castle, on the other hand, has an easier history to trace. The quintessential English castle, it is surrounded by 500 acres of woodland and set on two islands in the middle of a lake. Since its conception as a Saxon royal manor house in AD 857, it has been home to six medieval queens of England.

CASTLES

Arundel Castle (*right*) is the odd one out of these three; not only was it built much earlier, but it is also, as a traditional motte and double bailey castle, in a different style. Although it was begun in 1067 (to protect the gap that had been carved by the River Arun through the South Downs), most of what you see now is only a century old. After lying in ruins for fifty years after the civil war, it was lavishly renovated by various dukes of Norfolk in the 19th century.

Bodiam Castle (*left*) was built next in 1385, and Herstmonceux (*above*) in 1415. Today Hermonceux is an International Study Centre, the home of an annual Medieval Festival to raise funds for on-going maintenance and for other charities, 'as was the duty of all good Knights', and the romantic setting for modern day weddings, as in the photograph. Anyone interested in visiting the castle should be aware of the resident ghost!

HEVER CASTLE

Hever Castle (*left*) sprang into life when Edward I gave permission to Sir Stephen de Penchester to convert his house into a castle. Two hundred years later, the Bullen (or Boleyn) family bought the residence and gave it a face-lift, building a comfortable Tudor home within the walls. The family's most famous offspring, and the second wife of Henry VIII, was Anne Boleyn, who grew up here; and here too Henry's fourth wife, Anne of Cleves, lived after their divorce. In 1903, the Castle was bought by William Waldorf Astor, an American millionaire, who set about restoring the original structure as well as developing the gardens and lake.

BODIAM CASTLE

Although the Domesday Book documents a Saxon hall near this site, Bodiam Castle (*right*) was actually built by Sir Edward Dalyngrigge, as a defence against impending French forces. Although the invasion never took place, the castle was passed through many hands over the years and was pretty much neglected until 1917. The interior is ruined, but the exterior, sounded by a wide moat, looks like a fairytale castle and it is easy to imagine that it was an intimidating deterrent. The small islet that remains was once part of a strategically placed network of bridges and paths, ensuring that access to the castle was both difficult and dangerous.

DOVER CASTLE

Dover Castle (*left*) occupies such a strongly positioned defensive site that it was in continuous military use until the 1980s, although its origins date back to the 12th century. Henry II spent the then enormous sum of £7,000 building the castle on the site of an Iron Age fort. Within the walls are the remains of a Roman lighthouse (Pharos – among the tallest Roman structures still standing in Europe) and an Anglo-Saxon church. Perhaps the most exciting and unusual features of this castle are the secret wartime tunnels, built underground during the Napoleonic wars.

SALTWOOD CASTLE

Like so many other castles, Saltwood (*right*) is associated with one infamous event above all others: the fatal quarrel between Henry II and Thomas Beckett. Although back in the 12th century the castle technically belonged to the Archbishopric of Canterbury, the King allowed one of his more aggressive barons, Rannulf de Broc, to live there with his private army despite Beckett's frequent protests. The men's loyalty was well publicised, and so Saltwood was the rendezvous-point for the four knights who conspired to murder Beckett and win the King's favour.

PORTCHESTER CASTLE

The best preserved site of a Roman fort in Northern Europe, Portchester Castle (*left*) spans almost two thousands years of occupation. Some time around 280 AD, the Romans enclosed nine acres of this integral headland in walls 20 feet high and 10 feet thick (although the depth was quickly reduced when local people began stealing the stones for their own buildings!) Since then, it's prime position for defending Portsmouth Harbour has meant constant and varied use, from Roman fort to medieval stronghold to royal palace to prison.

SISSINGHURST GARDENS

Although Sissinghurst Castle (*right*) was once famous for having entertained Queen Elizabeth, it was used as a jail for around 3,000 French prisoners during the Seven Years War, and suffered decades of neglect. When Harold Nicolson and his wife, the writer and poet Vita Sackville-West, bought the castle in 1930, they effectively bought a workhouse – the only part left standing. However the couple quickly restored what they could of the house and set about creating the Elizabethan-style garden for which the area is now renowned.

MAZES

Maze-maker extraordinaire Adrian Fisher designed both the mazes that we see here. The maze at Leeds Castle (*above*) was part of a project set up in 1974 by Lady Baillie, the last private owner of the castle. She wanted to encourage the arts as well as maintaining the property and the garden. Opened to the public on 25 May 1988, it is designed with a royal theme in mind; from the stone in the centre of the maze you can see a queen's crown and chalice.

While the first is a hedge maze, the photograph on the left shows a maize maze. Situated at Tulley's Farm, near Crawley, it is part of a collection of mazes created in 2000 called 'Castles in the Clouds'. It is unsurprising, therefore, that in this maze you can see the shapes of clouds as well as a castle.

TOWNS AND VILLAGES

Of all the towns and villages in south-east England, Canterbury is undoubtedly the most famous. It has had a somewhat chequered history, starting as a Belgic settlement that was overrun by the Romans, and then, after the Empire's collapse in the 6th century, by the Saxons who renamed it Cantwarabyrig. It was during the Saxon period that Augustine came to Canterbury, on a mission from the Pope to convert the British Isles to Christianity. During his stay, Augustine founded two Benedictine monasteries, one of which later became the first cathedral in England – Christ Church. The new religion soon turned into a power struggle between the abbots from the monasteries, the archbishops and the monarch, eventually resulting in the murder of Thomas Becket.

Canterbury might boast Roman and early Christian ruins, a Norman castle, and an extremely famous cathedral, it might have been the birthplace of Chaucer's *Canterbury Tales* and Rupert Bear; but the most dramatic changes have been in the last 60 years. Right on the flight path from London during the Second World War, and Cathedral's Bell Tower, it was an ideal place for German raiders to drop any unused bombs before flying home across the Channel. It was also a target for the notorious Baedeker Raids, with a third of the city being destroyed in one particular raid in 1942.

History, as well as the war, has left its mark on more of the south east than just Canterbury. Its proximity to the coast has meant that Roman occupation is clear. In Chichester, for example, the layout of the town, the city walls, the centre and its four main streets closely resemble the original. There is also a Roman villa at Lullingstone, seven miles north of Sevenoaks, with some of the best-preserved Roman mosaics on show, including a spectacular floor depicting the Chimera, a fire-breathing creature with a lion's head, a goat's body and a serpent's tail. A recent excavation of a nearby chamber turned up early Christian iconography, implying that the villa may have been used as a Romano-Christian chapel in the third century. If this were true, it would have pre-empted the official arrival of Christianity by three hundred years, and would make Lullingstone one of the earliest sites of clandestine Christian worship in England.

Regardless of the past, it must not be forgotten that these are primarily places where people simply live. Aerial photography is often at its most impactful when offering a rarely seen view of a place you know, so take a look at the following pictures and perhaps you will even be able to see your own back garden!

CANTERBURY

Above The beautiful moated manor house of Ightham Mote, nestling in a sunken valley, was built in 1340. The doorway is original, although the oriel window was put in later, as was the gatehouse tower. Surrounded by a wealth of supernatural stories, including one about real skeletons in a cupboard, it was in danger of demolition until a programme of restoration was started in 1988. *Left* is a panoramic view of the second most visited place in Britain, Canterbury.

ST AUGUSTINE'S ABBEY

Just across the road from Canterbury Cathedral stands St Augustine's Abbey (*left*), occupying the site of a church founded by St Augustine in 598. At the bottom left hand corner of this photograph is the entrance to the College, once known as Fyndon Gate. It was named after Abbot Fyndon who built it in the early 14th century, but is now simply referred to as Main Gate. It has been significantly restored after damage in the war, and is now in the ownership of King's School, previously part of the 19th-century St Augustine's Missionary College.

CANTERBURY CATHEDRAL

Saxon remains were discovered at this site in an archaeological dig in 1993, although the Cathedral (*right*) has clearly undergone many facelifts since the Dark Ages. It has become notorious for one event above all others – Thomas Beckett's murder in 1170. Days after he died, reports of miracles began to spread throughout England, and soon the tomb was a mecca for pilgrims. Today the Cathedral attracts around 2 million visitors every year, and they can see a groove in the marble floor up the stairs where the pilgrims of the 12th century entered on their knees, and remained on them, as they worshipped at his shrine.

MAIDSTONE

Already an active settlement, called 'Meddestane', in the 11th century, Maidstone's name means 'the people's stone'. The first recorded trial in England was held here, and it is more than likely that a stone marked the place of the 'moot' or county assembly. Standing on the Rivers Medway and Len, Maidstone was a natural market centre from which fruit and vegetables were shipped to London, and that role continues today. The area is also the main source of hops for brewing.

ROYAL TUNBRIDGE WELLS

Tunbridge Wells was nothing more than a forest until it was 'discovered' in 1606. A young nobleman, Lord North, stopped to drink from a spring. Realising that the water contained iron, he took a sample back to London and soon Tunbridge Wells was transformed into a fashionable health spa. It was especially popular amongst royalty, who believed the water's medicinal qualities would aid recovery from the excesses of court life. The town was built around the spring by enterprising locals, who identified the need for accommodation; when Queen Henrietta Maria, the wife of Charles I, arrived to take the spa water, she had to camp in tents on the common.

SEVENOAKS

It is unclear whether or not the seven oaks in the name ever existed in the past, but trees from Knole Park were planted with great ceremony in 1955 ... and then destroyed in the great storm of October 1987. Sevenoaks is most famous for Knole House, as seen on the front cover of this book. Designed to match the calendar numerically, with 7 courtyards, 52 staircases and 365 rooms, it has been home to archbishops of Canterbury and royalty, and was the birthplace of Vita Sackville-West.

WESTERHAM

Situated between two upland areas – the North Downs to the north and the Greensand Ridge just to the south, Westerham is so named because it is one of the most westerly towns in Kent. The town was the birthplace of James Wolfe, who fought and won the decisive Battle of Quebec between the English and the French in 1759. His statue stands alongside one of Winston Churchill, whose country home, Chartwell, lies just outside town.

CHICHESTER

In the 1st Century AD, Chichester (*left*) was selected as the base camp of the invading Romans. 2000 years later, one of their remnants turned out to be one of the most exciting archaeological discoveries made for decades. In 1960, when workmen were laying a waterpipe, they found a mosaic floor which was later identified as the largest single Roman building found in Britain so far – so large, in fact, that the original building would have competed with the palaces of Imperial Rome itself. These days it is the Cathedral that overshadows the rest of the town.

HORSHAM

Horsham takes its name from a Saxon term meaning *horse pasture*, and was originally a country market town. The town was at its most prosperous between 1300 and 1830, when it took turns with Lewes and Chichester to hold the county assizes. These events attracted large numbers of spectators and the town would take on a carnival atmosphere.

Close to Horsham is St Leonard's Forest, encompassing 12,000 acres. According to legend, the lilies of the valley covering the forest bed sprang up from drops of blood shed by St Leonard after fighting a mighty dragon.

HORSHAM AND ARUNDEL

Arundel (*right*) has been a settlement since pre-Roman times, and lying at a strategically important point – where the east-west land route through Sussex crosses the River Arun, it was an important port and market town. It has three major sites, a castle (see page 33), a cathedral and a church that dates back to the 14th century. Also a market town, Horsham (*left*) was founded in the mid-10th century and many public executions took place here by method of 'death by compression', when stones would be placed on the criminal's chest until he was crushed.

GUILDFORD

Guildford (*left*) has been the capital of the region since pre-Norman times and in the 10th century even had its own mint. The road pattern, clearly seen from the air, was established during this time and remains basically unchanged today. Now in ruins, Guildford Castle was built by Henry II as a royal residence in the 12th century, although 200 years later it was being used as the main jail for the county of Sussex. Just down the hill from the castle is a statue of Alice in Wonderland, to commemorate the Rev Charles Dodgson, aka Lewis Carroll, who lived here for some years.

EAST GRINSTEAD

Like Guildford, East Grinstead's economy went into decline as the wool trade began to fail. So it made use of its location – halfway between Portsmouth and London – and became a popular stopping-place for travellers, overnight or for a midday meal as roads got better. The Church of St Swithun, which can be seen clearly above the rest of the buildings, was originally a 14th-century building with two towers. One was hit by lightening in 1683 and the other collapsed in 1785. The churchyard contains graves going back over 500 years, including those of three Protestant martyrs burned at the stake in the market place in 1556.

COASTLINE

THE STRETCH OF COASTLINE from the Thames Estuary to the Isle of Wight is arguably the most famous in Britain. Because of its closeness to France it has been the preferred landing point of invading forces from Julius Caesar to William the Conqueror to Hitler, and in consequence has been extensively redeveloped over the centuries with a series of defensive sites to guard against attack. Although some precautionary measures have been as simple as slicing a pier into small segments, the largest defence programme since Saxon times happened after Henry VIII divorced Catherine of Aragon. England was left so politically isolated that whispers of a treaty between France and Spain were enough to arouse fears of an invasion. Although the threat was short-lived, it inspired Henry to commission around 30 Device Forts, of which ten survive today. These squat, cylindrical towers can be still be seen at Walmer, Deal Castle and Sandgate, among others.

As you would expect, the water has always been used as a mode of transport, especially for the export of wool and later cloth in the middle ages. It was perhaps during this time that the area was at it's most influential. The Cinque Ports in particular brought a sense of autonomy, as well as royally sanctioned importance. And with so many enclosed bays and inlets difficult to access, this part of the coastline has a long tradition of smuggling – another prosperous pastime.

Today, of course, the southeast of England is an international gateway to the rest of the country. The busy Dover and Folkestone ports whisk people back and forth to France, as does the Channel Tunnel. The sheer choice of beaches has meant that all manner of holiday resorts have sprung up, from trendy Brighton to the traditionally less dynamic Worthing and Bognor Regis. The closure of many ports may have reduced commercial traffic, but the water remains an ideal place for amateur sailing. In other words, from transport and industry to rest and relaxation, the water has shaped the history of the surrounding counties, just as it has physically shifted and eroded the shape of the shoreline.

COALHOUSE FORT AND THE RIVER MEDWAY

Left On the north bank of the Thames near East Tilbury, Coalhouse Fort is considered by many to be the finest surviving example of an armoured casement fort in the UK. Built during the Victorian era along with over 70 other forts around the British coastline, it was completed in 1874. With its sister forts, Cliffe and Shenmead, it guarded the approach to London by river.

Above The neigbouring River Medway is now a popular place to go sailing.

TILBURY DOCKS

Looking East down the River Thames, Tilbury has one of the only remaining ports here since the closure of all the main docks around Canary Wharf in the 1960s and 1970s. The docks were first built in 1882 and are now used as the main container port for London. The huge Shell Havern Oil Refinery ceased production in December 1999, but is due to be regenerated as a flagship port, thanks to a partnership between Shell and P&O.

QUEEN ELIZABETH BRIDGE

Opened in 1991, the Queen Elizabeth Bridge was built over a three-year period and cost £86 million. Measuring 450 metres in length, it is Europe's largest cable-supported bridge, and the tolls that the southbound traffic brings goes back to the corporations which funded the project. Further down the Thames, towards the sprawling estuary, are winding banks – a place of personal significance to our photographer, Jason Hawkes: it was here twelve years ago that he joined a microlight club, and first took to the skies.

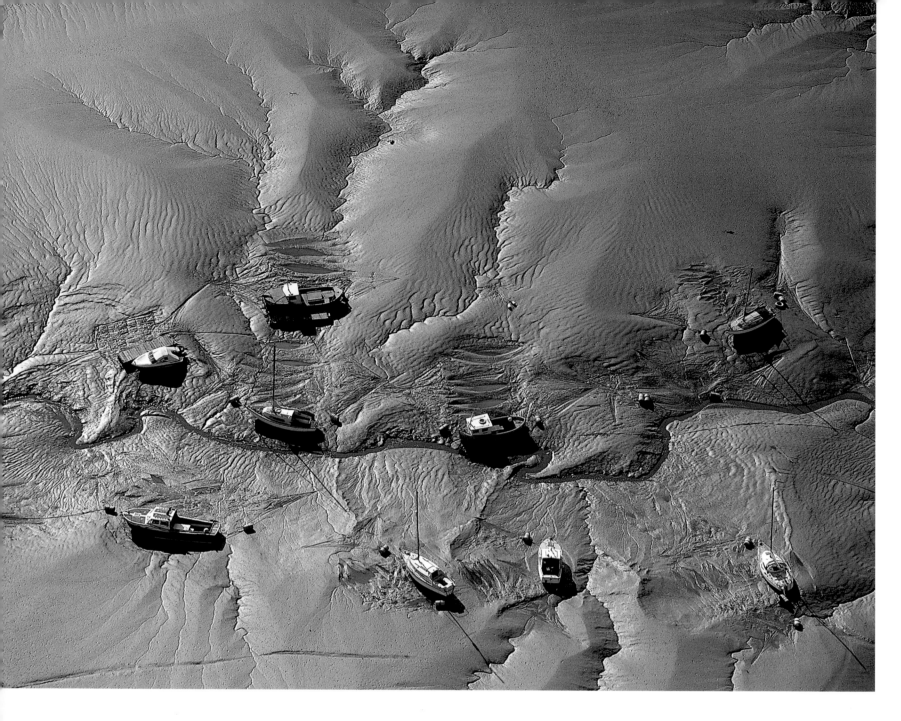

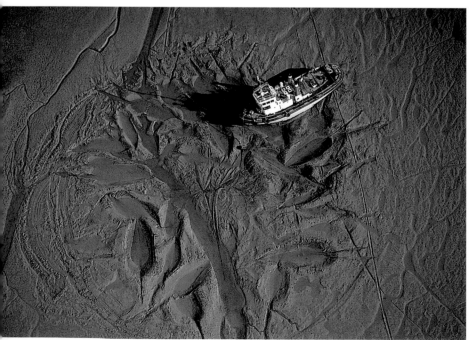

ROCHESTER AND CHATHAM, KENT

The historic dockyards at Chatham and the River Medway have been the backdrop to many infamous men and events. Previously an unknown village, Chatham was transformed when Elizabeth I ordered the building of a dockyard. It was here that many of the ships that routed the Spanish Armada in 1588 were built; and when one of the fleet's commanders, Vice Admiral Sir Francis Drake, was an apprentice, he learned his seamanship on the Medway. In 1771, a twelve-year-old boy called Horatio Nelson arrived to join the *Raisonnable*. Perhaps he glimpsed into his future and saw the HMS *Victory* moored in the Medway. Almost 50 years later, John Dickens joined the Naval Pay office, and brought with him his son Charles, who grew up to write some very unflattering things about Chatham.

In the foreground (*right*) is Rochester which, having provided the setting for various parts of *Great Expectations* and *The Pickwick Papers*, now makes the most of its connection with Dickens. A festival is held each year to commemorate him.

WHITSTABLE

In 1830, Whitstable was appointed the northern terminal for the 'Crab and Winkle' line – Britain's first steam-powered passenger railway service. A popular holiday resort, it had been famous for almost 2,000 years before this on account of its oysters. At the height of its popularity in the 1950s, oyster beds covered 5,000 acres off-shore. Although oyster dredgers collecting the 'Royal Whitstable Natives' are still a common sight, today sea pollution has meant that it is less prosperous than in its heyday.

Dover cliffs

Dover has a long and well-documented history, dating back 6,000 years to the Stone Age and firmly entwined with the sea. The town has changed shape and size many times over the centuries, due to erosion and changing water levels, and much of the earliest remains are thought to have been destroyed. We do know that Dover's first inhabitants crossed the Channel by boat and brought with them corn seed and domesticated animals. One of the first known shipwrecks in Britain also occurred just off the coast of Dover during the Bronze Age, leaving tools and weapons strewn all over the seabed, and providing archaeologists with vital clues about how our ancient ancestors lived.

DOVER CLIFFS

The first serious invasion of Britain took place in August 55 BC. The exact point where Julius Caesar and his army landed is unknown, due to the ever-changing shoreline; it was certainly very close to Dover, probably on the welcoming beaches between Walmer and Deal, but definitely not Dover itself, although this was Caesar's first choice. The reason? The legendary white cliffs, which acted as a beacon to the Roman soldiers as they crossed the water but also as a powerful deterrent when they arrived.

DOVER PORT

Over 12 million people visit Dover each year, mainly for the most notorious of all its attractions; the busy passenger port. Dover owes its significance to the proximity of France, 21 miles to Calais and 25 miles to Bologne, and this in itself has made the port an important maritime trading centre since the Bronze Age. During the two World Wars, the port was especially active. In World War I, it was home to various warships and fishing vessels which ensured Britain's essential control of the channel, and in World War II it was a passage for the 200,000 men evacuated from Dunkirk who used the secret tunnels carved out of the cliffs.

Cliffs

'There'll be bluebirds over the white cliffs of Dover

Tomorrow, just you wait and see.'

The jagged, gleaming white cliffs of Dover (*left*) have contributed greatly to the region's history, immortalised in the wartime song, and regarded as a quintessential symbol of Englishness. On top of the cliffs you can find memorials to Louis Blerot, marking the site where he landed after making the first cross-channel flight in 1909, Captain Webb, the first man to swim the Channel in 1875, and C. S. Rolls, who made the first two-way flight across the Channel in 1910. One cliff, now referred to as Shakespeare Cliff, is even mentioned in *King Lear*, when Edward cries: '*...How fearful and dizzy 'tis to cast one's eyes so low!*'

Above A view of less extreme cliffs near Folkestone.

THE CHANNEL TUNNEL TERMINAL

The idea of the Channel Tunnel was originally conceived 160 years ago. A mile-long tunnel was carved out from

the English coast, but work was stopped by Queen Victoria who was worried about the possibility of invasion. The

project was revived in the late 1960s, and work started again in 1973 as a joint Anglo-French project. Today it is

possible to be whisked by train from London Waterloo to the Gard du Nord in Paris in just three and a half hours.

FOLKESTONE

On a clear day, the coast of France – just 26 miles away – can be seen from Folkestone, so it was a natural choice for the entry to the Channel Tunnel. Unusually for a seaside resort, there is no defined seafront as such. Instead there is the Leas, a mile and a half stretch of clifftop lawns, gardens, flower beds and a bandstand, running from the centre of town towards Sandgate to the west. One of England's most famous physicians, William Harvey, was born here in 1578. There is a statue of him near the Leas clutching a human heart, as one of his discoveries was the circulation of the blood. Unfortunately his discovery couldn't help him when it came to his own fate: he committed suicide in 1657 after he found out that he was going blind.

RYE

Set on a prominent hilltop site, Rye is partially ringed by the rivers Rother, Brede and Tillingham. Although in an easily defendable position, Rye was also the target for cross-channel raids; in 1377 almost every non-stone building was burned down in a ferocious French raid. It was added as a limb to the existing Cinque Ports in the 12th century, but suffered so badly from erosion and a receding coastline that a new port, Rye Harbour, had to be built. The silting up of the harbour led to a prolonged period of economic decline in Rye, but the upshot is that buildings that would have been rebuilt if the town had continued to be prosperous have survived. The most famous example is the Mermaid Inn, rebuilt in 1420 after the French raid 43 years before, later to become the headquarters of the Hawkhurst Gang of smugglers in the 18th century.

HASTINGS

Subject to many invading forces over the years, from cross-channel raids to flooding from the sea, Hastings will always be inextricably linked in people's minds with William the Conqueror and the Battle of Hastings. However, the conflict actually took place six miles inland, on a hill at Battle named Senlac, or the lake of blood.

Way before William, Hastings was a small Saxon town with a fishing harbour that became increasingly busy over the decades. As one of the original members of the Cinque Ports, the town really flourished in the 12th and 13th centuries, but it ran into problems when the harbour creek was silted up by the same storm that washed away nearby Winchelsea in 1287. Although the harbour is now buried underneath a modern shopping centre, the fishing industry managed to survive and one of the most characteristic sights are the tall, narrow huts used for drying nets and storing fishing tackle.

THE PIER AT HASTINGS

This amazing pier, a staggering 600 feet long, is certainly the focal point of the Hastings coastline, especially from the sea, or in our case, the air. Originally opened in 1872, it had to be cut in two places during World War II in order to prevent Hitler's forces from landing on it. It has since been repaired.

EASTBOURNE

After the arrival of the railway in 1849, Eastbourne grew from being literally open farmland to an elegant Georgian town lined with carefully planted rows of trees. Its stunning 8-mile sweep of coastline, overlooked by rolling green downlands, has attracted major praise. A possibly slightly biased John Aspden wrote in his 1978 Municipal History of the borough that, 'No British town has been more liberally endowed with the natural advantages of position and of climate.'

BEACHY HEAD

One of the most dramatic sights along this coastline, Beachy Head is a staggering 575 feet high. In comparison the offshore lighthouse looks like a child's toy, although it's beam can be seen from up to 16 miles away. As you can see, there is no beach (the name is derived from the French *beau chef*, meaning 'beautiful head'), just the stark chalk uplands where the sea has cut into the Sussex Downs. In the 18th century, this was a popular place for smugglers, who used to hide in freak clefts in the cliffs, such as Birling Gap.

SEAFORD

From the air, as well as from the ground, Seaford is another striking example of the dramatic coastline. Not only does the sandy beach stretch to Newhaven, 4 miles away, but the park, acclaimed as an 'area of outstanding natural beauty', is a haven for birdwatchers and wildlife. Like Rye, Seaford was appointed as a limb to the Cinque Ports in 1229 and was a busy port until the 16th century. Disease, floods and constant attacks from the French led to the decline of Seaford as a port, although local tradition states that it was a storm in 1579 that changed the course of the River Ouse, creating what is now known as Newhaven in the process. Seaford was left quite literally high and dry, and the inhabitants, deprived of their livelihoods, turned to less honourable ways of making a living. Thus the area became notorious for smuggling.

BRIGHTON

When Dr Richard Russell of Lewes published a paper on 'The Use of Sea Water in Diseases of the Glands', he transformed Brighton from a small fishing village into a fashionable seaside resort. Up until this point, people had used the Channel for fishing or to cross in order to fight the French. But to swim in? Never. All it took was a visit by the influential Prince of Wales and his social circle to seal Brighton's fate.

Just as fashionable today, Brighton is an eclectic mix of bohemian streets, outrageous architecture, buzzy nightlife and traditional seaside entertainment.

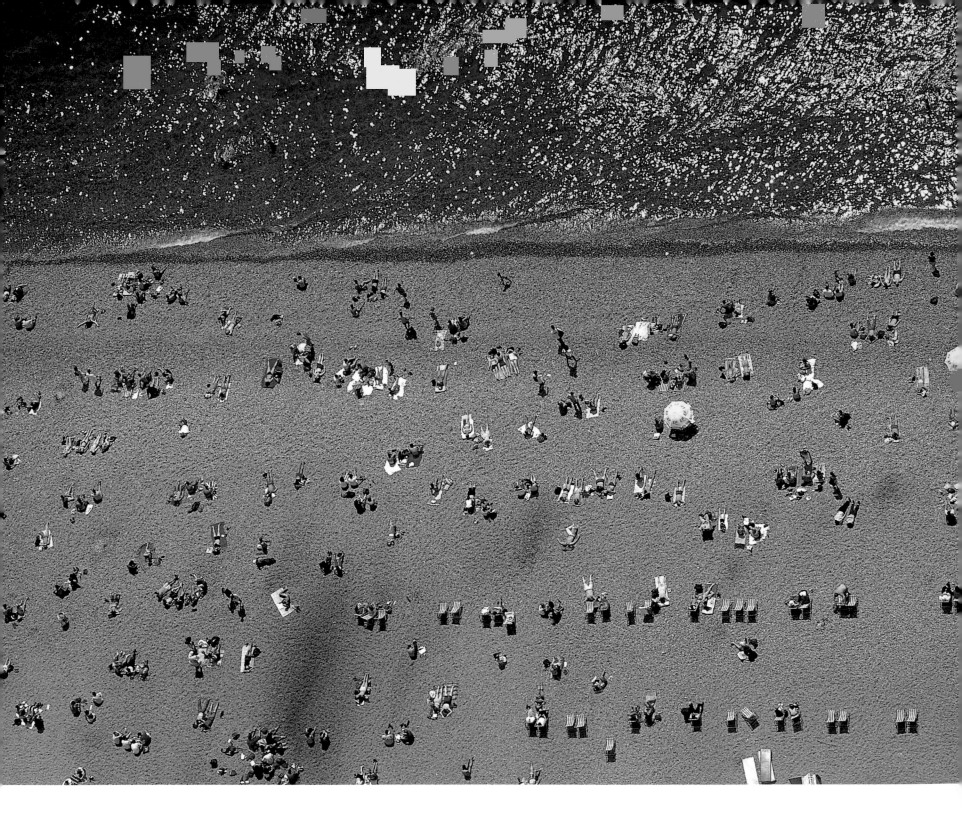

BRIGHTON BEACH

Brighton's reputation as a health resort grew to such an extent that, by the 19th century, bathing was its main source of business. Once the first train steamed into Brighton's station in 1841, the business boomed. Bathing machines littered the beach, and aristocrats were attended to by 'dippers', who ensured no one drowned. 150 years on, the beaches are still packed every summer with couples, students and families.

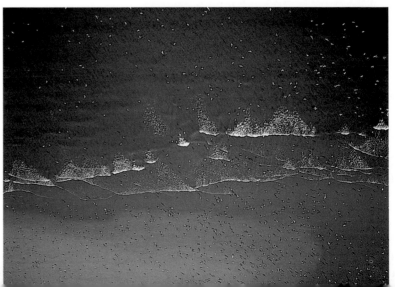

THE ROYAL PAVILION

The bizarre mismatch of architectural styles of the Royal Pavilion make it one of the most exotic-looking and best-loved buildings in the southeast of England. After starting life as a farmhouse, the Pavilion was taken in a classical direction by Henry Holland, and then given over to the Indian influences of John Nash. The result has not been to everyone's taste – a more cutting critic, William Cobbett, once described it as 'a square box, a large Norfolk turnip and four onions'!

BRIGHTON'S TWO PIERS

The bright-lights and candyfloss tackiness of the archetypal seaside resort is embodied on the Palace Pier. Packed full of tourists, every centimetre is dedicated to fun and moneymaking, from up-to-the-second video games to funfair rides and arcades. Half a mile along, Brighton's West Pier is no longer open to the public. Originally built in 1866, it was damaged in World War II and then fell into disrepair. However, thanks to Lottery funds, plans are in place to restore it to its former glory.

WORTHING

From humble beginnings – when first mentioned in the Domesday book, it had a population of just 22 – Worthing has grown to be the largest town in West Sussex, with a population of over 100,000. It was a simple fishing hamlet until Princess Amelia, youngest daughter of George III, visited it in 1798, and over the next 14 years Worthing expanded into a popular seaside resort. Traditionally the butt of comic's jokes due to its large population of pensioners, Worthing has had a lot of work carried out on the town centre in recent years and is stealing some of the thunder from neighbouring Brighton.

The town's pier, full of the traditional holiday attractions, dominates the stunning five-mile stretch of coastline and beautiful beaches. On a more cultural note, Worthing has two major literary connections. The poet Shelley's family were major landowners in this area, and Oscar Wilde wrote *The Importance of being Earnest* here, although the house he stayed in has long since been replaced by a block of flats.

GORING ON SEA

The road structure of Goring supports what the name suggests: the focus is very much on the sea, and it was once a small fishing village. A little-known fact about Goring on Sea: the church contains a replica of Michelangelo's Sistine Chapel ceiling.

BOGNOR REGIS

A London hatter transformed Bognor from a fishing hamlet to a seaside resort in 1787. Sir Richard Hotham wanted to attract the rich, famous and royal, to rival Brighton, and to rename the result Hothampton. During his lifetime, only the Prince of Wales made a visit. However his dream was realised posthumously when Bognor became Bognor Regis after King George V was brought here to convalesce from a serious illness in 1928.

BEWL WATER

Above Bewl Water is the largest area of open water in the South East: it holds up to 6,900 million gallons of water. As well as acting as a reservoir, supplying water to parts of Kent and Sussex, it also offers lots of activities, from walking and cycling to windsurfing, fly-fishing and sailing.

BOSHAM AND CHICHESTER HARBOURS

Legend has it that the grave of a child buried within the Holy Trinity Church in Bosham is King Canute's daughter, and that it was here that the Saxon King failed to turn back the incoming tide. True or not, Canute certainly visited Bosham with his father on a raid in 1049, and during one of these raids by the Danes the bells from the church were carried off as plunder. The galley carrying them struggled under their weight and sank to the bottom of the sea. Today it is said that whenever a peal is rung on the present bells, it is answered by a peal from the deep…

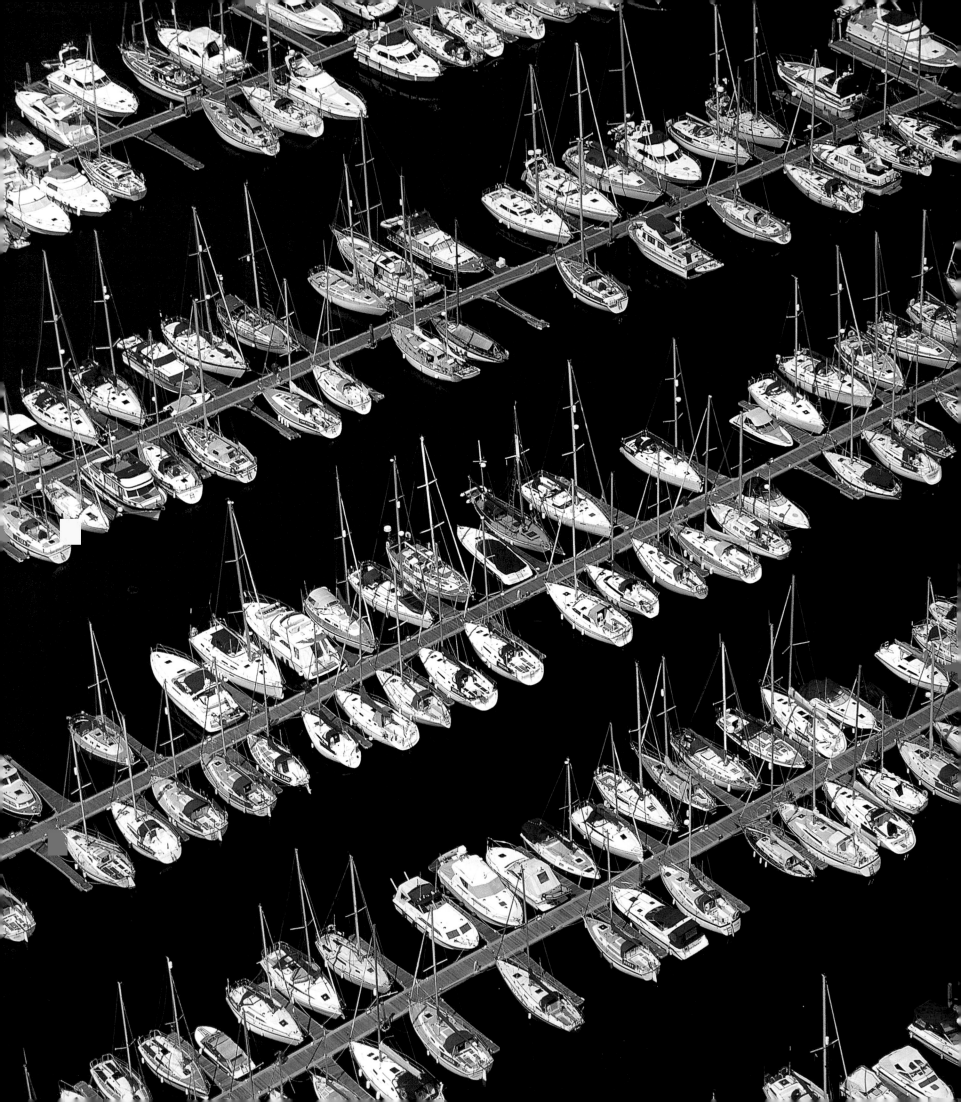

SAILING OFF THE COAST

Ever since the Romans first established a town at Chichester (Noviomagus), visiting ships have had to moor in the series of channels which spread inland from Hayling, as Chichester has no direct access to the sea. Although today the harbour has virtually no commercial traffic, it was extremely important throughout the middle ages in the exportation of goods, mainly wool and hides. By the 17th century, it was described as too dangerous to enter and an unfit place for a naval establishment. However, it made a comeback in the mid–18th century, primarily as a centre for shipbuilding, although the water mills and oyster beds hint at its wider industrial scope in earlier days. Today Chichester Harbour is an area of outstanding natural beauty, where people visit for leisure rather than industry.

Around Chichester Harbour

What was once a functional mode of transport has now become a source of pleasure and relaxation. Thousands of people flock to the semi-enclosed water of Chichester or the sea around Portsmouth to take advantage of the agreeable conditions for sailing. With 50 miles of shoreline and 17 miles of navigable water, Chichester harbour is a yachtsman's dream. This has been capitalised on thanks to the development of the extensive yacht basin at nearby Birham, and Chichester has fast become one of the busiest yachting centres in the British Isles.

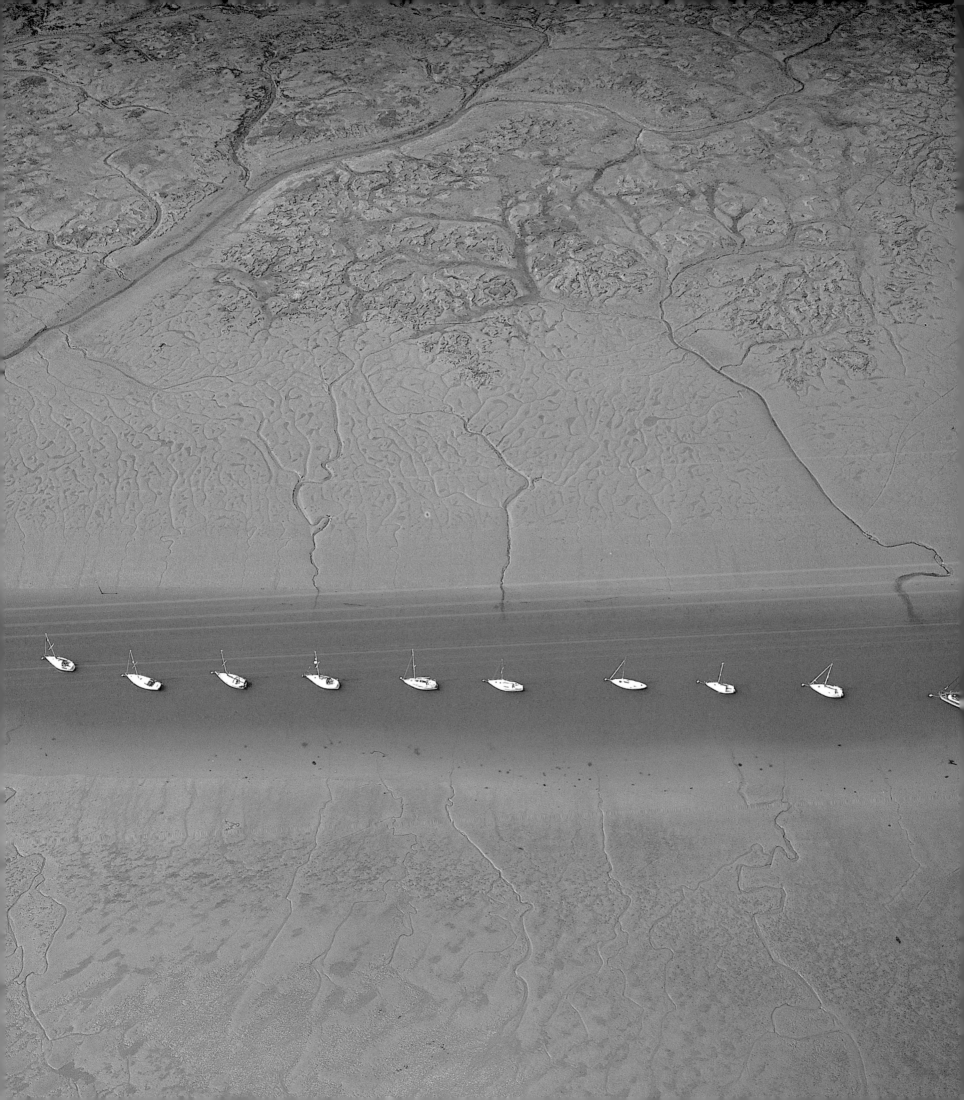

SEA AND SAND

The simple beauty of the coastline here at Bracklesham Bay
in West Sussex is irresistible. The water has coloured this
area's history, industry, leisure and traditions for centuries.

HAYLING ISLAND

Just 4 miles square, Hayling Island is a popular holiday
island whose freak formation divides the waters of
Langstone and Chichester Harbour. It is connected to
Havant, which has been a major road junction since
prehistoric times, by a bridge. In the background of this
picture you can clearly see Portsmouth Docks.

SOUTHSEA

Close to Southsea, the village of Beaulieu was once the site of an influential Cistercian monastery, which became famous for offering sanctuary to Queen Margaret of Anjou, amongst others. Built using stone from Caen and Quarr on the Isle of Wight, the abbey was dismantled after the Dissolution and the stone was used to build Southsea Castle. It is popularly believed that Henry VIII watched the *Mary Rose* sink from this vantagepoint.

As for literary connections, Ruyard Kipling spent six purportedly miserable years lodging in Southsea while his parents were in India. Furthermore, the first ever Sherlock Holmes book, *A Study in Scarlet*, was written here by Sir Arthur Conan Doyle, who also practised as a doctor in Elm Grove.

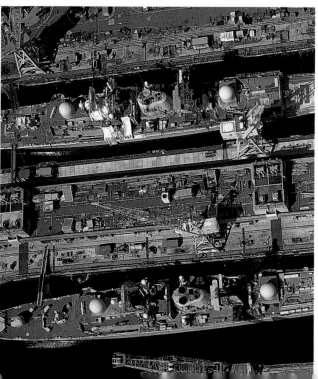

PORTSMOUTH DOCKS

When Sir Walter Raleigh landed in Camber Docks in Portsmouth Harbour after his voyage to the Americas, he brought back with him the first potatoes and tobacco ever seen in Britain. But Portsmouth has been better known as England's greatest naval station ever since Henry VII fortified the sea walls and built the country's first permanent dry dock behind them. The most famous of its heroes, Vice-Admiral Lord Nelson, took his last walk to Sally Port on 14 September 1805, where he boarded his barge and was rowed out to HMS *Victory*. Five weeks later he had smashed the Franco–Spanish fleet at Trafalgar and was dead. His flagship is now housed at the Maritime base, along with the *Mary Rose* and many new naval frigates. The naval theme is carried on in many attractions, including the Royal Navy Museum, opposite the *Victory* and the Submarine World in Gosport.

FAWLEY OIL REFINERY

Run by the Esso group, Fawley Oil Refinery is the largest of its kind in the country and is situated on Southampton water. Tankers carrying over 30,000 litres of fuel leave here daily, supplying up to 15 per cewnt of all the oil products used in the UK. However, most of the output is sent via vast underground pipes, measuring more than 1,200 km in total. Fawley pipes its product as far afield as Avonmouth, Birmingham and London, carrying up to 45 million litres a day.

SOUTHAMPTON

Southampton has a truly sea-faring history, and its port has been witness to some monumental events. It was from here that Henry V set sail for France to fight the Battle of Agincourt in 1415, the pilgrims embarked on the *Mayflower* on their journey to the New World in 1620, and the *Titanic* set off on its fatal voyage in 1912. The port suffered greatly during World War II as it was a prime target for raids, although many ancient buildings are still standing. A good example is Bargate, generally acclaimed as the finest medieval city gate in the country, and the principal entrance to Southampton between 1200 and 1930. Southampton Corporation trams had to be specially re-designed to pass through the gate, as its narrow archway was so low.

COWES

If Cowes (*right*) attracts the tourists, Sandown (*left*) caters for them. With every kind of seaside attraction, including the only surviving pleasure pier on the Isle of Wight, Sandown boasts miles of flat sands. In the distance you can see the coastline of England, 3 miles away. Cowes, the world-renowned yachting centre, started off as a shabby port whose main business was shipbuilding. When the Duke of Gloucester came to stay in 1811, the lack of entertainment on offer resulted in his watching sailing matches between local fishermen. The Duke's patronage led to enterprising locals founding a club and running their own races, which developed to such an extent that Cowes Week in August is now the premier yachting event of the year.

FRESHWATER BAY AND THE NEEDLES

If you had taken a stroll around Freshwater Bay 150 years ago, you might have bumped into the poet laureate, Alfred Lord Tennyson, a keen walker who lived nearby and who loved to wander around the bay. Although it used to be an inaccessible inlet popular with smugglers, today it is the base for cruises to the island's most spectacular natural feature, the Needles. Two of these jagged lines of gleaming chalk, towering up to 200 feet high, are known as Lord Holmes' Parlour and Kitchen, after a 17th-century governor of the island who once entertained his guests in the 'parlour' and kept his wines cool in the 'kitchen'.

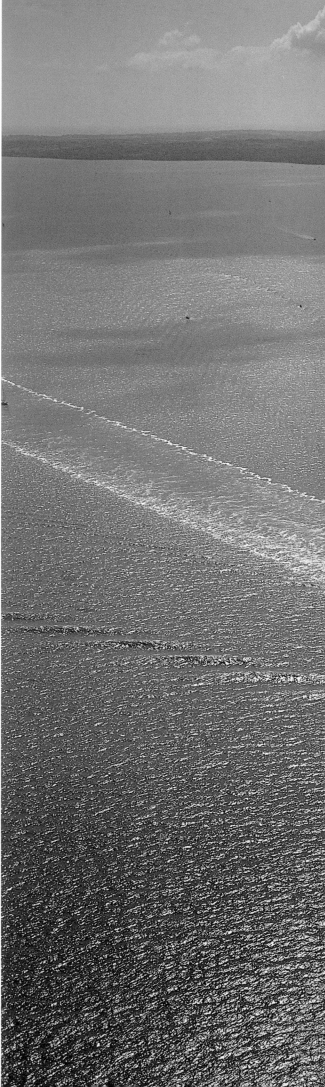

SPITBANK FORT

For 120 years, Spitbank Fort (above) has guarded the entrance to Portsmouth. Having survived the elements, two world wars and being the only sea fort open to the public, it remains almost completely intact. Make no mistake; this is a structure built to last. Divers had to position 35 feet of solid stone under the sea to form the foundations, and at basement level the solid granite walls are 15 feet thick. Inside, the fort is made up of a maze of passages and rooms, and a 400-foot deep well. With a capacity of 23,000 gallons a day, this is how fresh water was obtained while the Fort was in use. Today there are exhibitions showing how 156 men lived in the Fort at one time, sleeping in hammocks, using coal ranges, oil lamps and, of course, the well. There are replicas of the huge 38-ton guns, and some of the original shell and cartridge hoists are still in working order.

This P&O container ship (right) is probably on its way from one of the French ports to Southampton docks, and is pictured here just past Sandown on the Isle of Wight.

LEISURE AND PLEASURE

IF ITS R AND R you're after or a more exerting activity, the south-east has something for everyone. Famous for its mild climate, bracing air and astonishing variety of views, it is a paradise for walkers and nature lovers alike. The castles and forts that once played such a key role in defending this country are coming into their own once again these days for a very different reason – tourism. Many of them are now regarded as national treasures and are looked after by institutions such as the National Trust or English Heritage.

With the main resorts offering every conceivable seaside attraction, the golden stretches of sand will always act as a honey-pot for tourists. And after thousands of years of playing such a crucial role in this area, what a surprise to learn that today the water is also a source of leisure and pleasure for many people. Upstream the Arun is a good river for the angler, with an abundance of pike, perch, chub and roach. At weekends, the water around the mouth of the River Arun at Littlehampton and Chichester Harbour is crowded with yachts. Most

famous of all are the races: not only sailing at Cowes, but also horses at Goodwood and Epsom, and motor racing at Brand's Hatch.

It is somehow ironical that things that our ancestors depended on for survival, such as the castles and Cinque Ports which provided defence from foreign invasion, and the use of the water for transport, as well as the import and export of food, are now there for our enjoyment. The south-east may have been shaped by its past, but it is certainly not stuck in it: there is a plethora of redevelopments, including the huge shopping complex at Bluewater.

If you are inspired by these photographs, and fancy taking a look at the Garden of England from this exceptional perspective (and are not scared of heights!), there is a multitude of small airports and aerodromes in this region. Gaining access to fly alongside a landing plane at Gatwick (see page 127) may be a little hard to achieve, but there is a wealth of flying clubs and schools able to take you to the skies.

BLUEWATER

Bluewater (*left*) is reportedly Europe's largest shopping centre, and from the air you really get a sense of just how big it is. Covering an expansive 240 acres, it was built in March 1999 to offer an alternative to West End London high streets. And it seems to be working. Today around 80,000 people pass through the main doors to visit some of the 320 shops, restaurants and cinema screens that it encompasses.

From one extreme to the other, the solitary image of a rowing boat (*above*) on a lake close to Arundel Castle stands in stark contrast to the busy shopping centre.

EASTBOURNE

Who would have thought a simple caravan park (*right*) could ever have looked so striking? The coast will always come into its own during the summer months, when holidaymakers flock to the appealing beaches. At Redoubt Fortress (*above*), they hold open-air band concerts twice a week, followed by fireworks.

TIN CITY

Although it rather looks as if a nuclear bomb has exploded, destroying everything in its path bar this section of
a village, or possibly part of a set from Brookside or Coronation Street, Tin City actually belongs to the army.
Near West Hythe, the fake village is used as a training ground for troops going to Northern Ireland. Attention
to detail is so exact that if you look closely you will be able to see the same shop signs you would find in your
local high street.

CIRCULAR HOUSING

Perhaps beauty in the mundane is one of the criteria for good design. After all, the Bauhaus school of architecture decrees that form must follow function. It is easy enough to imagine an architect slumped over a drawing board, working out the finer points for this project, but I wonder if they ever got to see it from the air, apart from in their mind's eye?

Goodwood Racecourse

The 'Glorious Goodwood' meeting, starting on the last Tuesday of every July, is among the main events in the racing calendar. This famous racecourse takes its name from Goodwood House, a fine Georgian mansion overlooking the racecourse. The Duke of Richmond, one of King Charles II's illegitimate children, bought the 1000-acre estate in 1697. In 1750 the King's great-grandson, an immensely rich ambassador to the French court at Versailles, inherited it. He increased the Goodwood estate to 17,000 acres, built a huge stable block and introduced the horse racing for which Goodwood is now famous. Unfortunately, his investment proved disastrous and by the time of his death the estate had debts of £180,000.

EPSOM RACECOURSE

Another well-known racing centre is Epsom. Each year sees the arrival of thousands of enthusiasts come to watch the annual Epsom Derby, and to have a go on the funfair. Although informal racing took place as early as 1683, it was formalised in 1779 when a party of aristocrats established a race, later to be named after one of the party, Lord Derby.

BRANDS HATCH

As far as motor racing is concerned, Brands Hatch is one of the premier spectator tracks in the world. The original layout has not greatly changed since its original conception as a grass track circuit in 1926, but it was covered in asphalt in the 1950s.

SPORTS DAY AND READING FESTIVAL

Everyone can remember their school sports day, whether it was the humiliation of coming last in the sack race or the triumph of coming first in the egg and spoon. Traditionally watched by doting parents, the real joy or disaster of the day for the kids always seemed to rest on how well Mum and Dad did in their respective races!

Second only to Glastonbury, Reading Festival has a legendary reputation with music lovers from their mid-teens upwards. Held over the August Bank Holiday weekend each year, this music festival attracts some of the biggest names from independent and alternative labels. Camping is *de rigueur*, as you can see from the photograph.

THE M25 AND GATWICK AIRPORT

Best known for its traffic jams, the M25 is reduced to Scalectrix proportions from the air. Built to contain the flow of traffic, it has resulted in exacerbating the problem by encouraging more motorists to take to the road. After our journey though the landscape and history of the south-east of England, it is appropriate that we should end with pictures of modern modes of transport. Where once water was the gateway to the rest of the world, today everything is happening in the air!

INDEX